Con/*verse*/sations

with

Myself

A Collection of Poems

Con/*verse*/sations
with
Myself

A Collection of Poems

By Mike Orlock

Four Windows Press

231 N Hudson Ave., Sturgeon Bay, WI 54235

Con/*verse*/sations with *My*self

Copyright © 2021 Mike Orlock

Published by Four Windows Press, Sturgeon Bay, Wisconsin. All rights reserved. No part of this book may be reproduced without the author's written permission, except for brief quotations in reviews.
www.fourwindowspress1.com

Printed in the United States of America by Ingram Sparks

Book Layout © BookDesignTemplates.com

Library of Congress Cataloging-in-Publication Data available on request

ISBN

for my granddaughters

Kapri

Kayla

Rori

Rosi

&

Addie Mae

Acknowledgments

Photography by Liz Orlock.

The following poems have previously appeared in print or on-line publications: "Sailing to Mar-a-lago" (*Bramble*, 2021); "Uncertain Spring" (Wisconsin Writers Association Jade Ring, 2020); "Everything Empties and Refills" (*Your Daily Poem* website, 2021); "You Say Tomato, I Say" (*Your Daily Poem* website, 2018); "Beautiful Magic" (*Your Daily Poem* website, 2021).

Other Books by the Author

You Can Get Here from There: Poems of Door County & Other Places

Poetry Apocalypse & Selected Verse

Mr. President! Poetry, Polemics & Fan Mail from Inside the Divide

Table of Contents

Beginnings

A Legal Disclaimer

Dear Reader,
before entering into this written arrangement,
we should review the terms
that apply to the transaction
we are about to undertake
in order to make this interaction
as pleasurable as possible for both of us.

Despite existing as a documented text,
this poem is not an aesthetically binding contract.
It is instead a kind of pollicitation,
a promise made conventional
with words and versification.
It exchanges my ideas for your time
in an informal way as old as the act
of vocal recitation around
the first fires in communal caves,
when language became currency
and poetry intentional in the marketplace
of usefully diverting digressions.

You give me your attention, Reader,
this agreement loosely stipulates,
to reason through my convoluted tropes
and rhyme, and I will reciprocate best I can
by plucking words from my head
and pulling metaphors out my ass,
(forgive the expression)
to amuse you in ways you might
never have imagined or expected,
with the implicit understanding
I have something to say worth saying,
perfected through long hours of revision
and excision in order to keep
my end of our bargain beneficial.

In no way does my failure to fulfill
whatever expectations you have
for the quality of my work leave me
liable to actual action other than review.
Nor do I assume any responsibility
for the detrimental effects my words
or craft might have upon your metaphysics,
be they philosophical or emotional.
If not completely satisfied after sampling
from the smorgasbord of my oeuvre,
you will have to suffice yourself
with condemning me in the court
of public opinion, where the slings and arrows
of critical judgment await those Poets
fortunate enough to have had their work
consumed, digested, and rejected
by Readers who actually took the time
to consider it before dismissing it
(rather than ignoring it completely).

Until then, I remain, humbly,
if not anonymously, your hopeful Scribe.

Ours, Poetica

Who will write poems, asks the world in its churning,
with verses that pulse of our struggles and yearning?
Who will fit words into puzzles of sound,
and measure the meter that wraps the day round?

We'll trope the trees, say the birds in their chirping.
These limbs and these leaves will be ours for the parsing.
Their sap is the ink that makes quills of our feathers,
their roots the syntax that holds things together.
But can a tree be a poem when it stands against time,
wordlessly watching the stars in the sky?
Can a tree do the things that a poem ought to do —
squeeze a forest of life into a haiku?

I'll rhyme the flowers, says the grass in its greening.
They'll give the depth that colors my meaning.
I'll revise and refine my fields for them;
I will cherish and nurture each petal and stem.
Their reds and their pinks, their yellows and blues; their violets,
purples, whites and chartreuse make vibrant and beautiful conceits,
it is true, but mustn't a poem be more than mere hue?
Shouldn't it dance in splinters of light to dazzle the day and sparkle the
        night?
Can a flower be more than a color defined?
Can it blossom the heart and garden the mind?

I will couplet the clouds, says the wind in its zephyrs.
I will push and pull them across the wide heavens.
I will make them personify the moods of the moment,
give voice to their feelings in the storms they will foment.
The rain might be metaphor, but the sky is no page
to wax about beauty and rhapsodize rage.
A poem must move more than shadows and shapes,
should be more than the sum of its meters and feet.
A cloud is a cloud is a cloud, I contend,
but a poem's not a poem without a poet at hand.

Then I will cull such ones, says the world in reply, those that can see

with more than their eyes; and who feel without fingers and taste without
    tongues;
and who hear with their hearts the sounds of our songs.
For a world without poetry would be words without end, like sky
without clouds, empty of wind; or grass without flowers and birds
without trees, a world without music lifted by leaves.
Think silence, think stillness, think passion unstirred —
without poetry there to both soothe and disturb.
Such makers of words we shall know as our own,
and what's planted within them will grow into poems.

Gun Gab & Trump Talk

NRA Bible Story

In the beginning, God created the world we would die in
and creatures great and small we could kill;
and He created Man in His image and likeness;
but the world was a quiet place, without conflict
and competition, without thought and prayer.
So God said, "Let there be Gun,"
and there was Gun. And God saw that Gun was good
but incomplete; so God made for Gun, Bullet,
that Gun would have dominion over Man
and Man would have dominion over all the beasts
of the world. And He said to Man, "Behold,
I have given you the tool to your salvation,
the instrument of your survival, an inalienable right
granted by Me and protected by second amendment
to My sixth Commandment of ten,
which I haven't released yet but am currently revising.
So thou can go forth and shoot, and in My name, kill."
And Man did.
And there were many thoughts and prayers.
And God was pleased.

The Arms of God

"We have some different beliefs up north. We tend to be a little more conservative. We like our guns. We believe in God."
Sheriff Dan Miller, Florence County WI

And God believes in you, too, Sheriff,
and He loves His guns.
He owns several.
His favorites are a Sig Sauer
P320 RX with a black polymer grip
that fits snugly in His divine hands
and a DB15 M4 Carbine AR-15
semi-automatic rifle with a free float
quad rail hand guard
and collapsible stock
that the Almighty considers
absolutely indispensable for exercising
His celestial omnipotence.

There's no getting around it:
The universe is a dangerous place.
It's getting more dangerous by the parsec.
The only security a Deity can count on
when exploring those blackest holes
even heavenly light avoids
is the heat He can legally pack
thanks to His Second Commandment,
Thou shalt not abridge My right to bear arms.

If there's going to be a Big Bang II,
you better believe
God will be ready.

Gun Proud and Loud

There is so much demonization of guns by public schools…, but a kid can't wear a shirt showing his gun pride?

> — Nik Clark, WI Carry Inc.
> explaining his group's involvement in a lawsuit
> Green Bay Press Gazette Feb. 24, 2020

Pride in guns should never be abridged, Mr. Clark
maintains, for guns have much of which to be proud,
any true student of the Second Amendment
can explain. Think of all that guns have accomplished,
what good they have done
bringing people together, so it is only fitting
to glorify the story of the gun in what we wear.
Even a lowly .22 caliber can roar
loudly as any .357 Magnum
(as recorded one March morning two decades ago
by a student at Santana High in Santee, California)
pridefully proving size doesn't really matter
in matters of brain matter and blood spatter.
Little can be as lethal as large,
and what better way to celebrate our rights,
what finer means to commemorate the pride
one feels for the special guns in this fight
than to wear one on a tee shirt for all the school to see,
to demonstrate proudly and loudly
This is me?

Insurrection Day

January 6, 2021

The Fat Man promised it would be wild.
Come to Washington, he said,
bring a date and your hate.
Junior will be there.
Rudy, too.
We'll gather on the Ellipse
just outside the White House,
my house, he said,
and we'll steal back what was stolen,
and we'll march, Man, banners waving
and fists clenched, voices raving
and boots jacked — and if
blood has to spill, remember:
It's not a party till somebody's bleeding.
So come to D.C., he said,
it will be historic!
The world will be watching!
We'll be on TV!

So, we came as he directed,
and we listened and we seethed.
We cheered and hollered
through the warm-up acts,
Junior and Roger, Rudy G.
They worked hard to get us juiced,
but we knew where we were headed,
what we were expected to do.
When he finally took the stage
to speak sometime around noon,
the Fat Man looked resplendent,
a vision in navy blue, face glowing
with a radioactive sheen.
From behind bullet-proof glass
he promised: he'd lead us down
Pennsylvania every step of the way.
But his bone spurs must've acted up.
When we got there he was nowhere
seen. We had to do what he wanted

by ourselves. He had to watch things
on TV.

The Capitol looked like a postcard,
white and imposing and grand.
Cops had erected barricades around it,
as if they expected a mob.
A few of them got riled
when we pushed and shoved
them aside, but most just stood
and watched us as we surged
past them to get inside.
Some doors were broken,
some windows smashed,
some desks were ransacked,
some papers snatched.
Patriots snapped selfies
of themselves and their friends,
standing at the Speaker's lectern
like they were giving speeches,
debating laws they could pass
the rest of us would break.

It was everything the Fat Man said
it would be — and more.
How often do you get an invitation
to ransack the store?
We heard some gunshots
that sounded like fireworks popping,
smelled some gas that burned
a bit before stopping, learned later
some people died on the day,
but just five so that ain't shit.
You have to expect it
when you're insurrecting
to restore democracy
and the rule of law.
Things might get a little messy.
That's the American way, after all.

Just Asking (Hypothetically Speaking)

Hypothetical ? #1

So you're a Muslim *jihadi*
mad for martyrdom and the express ticket to Paradise promised in the
    program
which is why you strap thirty sticks of dynamite to your waist
and blow yourself and some unlucky others to smithereens in the local
    market
because you're expecting to be greeted by no fewer than 72 vestal virgins
    (count 'em!)
there on the other side of the pearly gates
welcoming you like you're the hottest beefcake in the afterlife.
Are you disappointed if there are, say, only 55 awaiting you?
Disillusioned if it's 20?
What happens to your bedrock belief system if
the only thing you find in the heavenly vapor is 72 other gullible losers
    like you,
each thinking maybe *you're* the virgin *he's* been promised?
Do you spend the rest of eternity together
wondering, *WTF was I thinking?*

Hypothetical ? #2

So, you're some white kid
steeped in the toxic tea of white supremacy
convinced that 16 million Twitter tweeters can't be wrong
that there really *is* an invasion of black and brown people out to steal
    your place
in line at the McDonald's drive-thru
and it's up to *you* to make like the Minutemen of old (be bold!)
grab your AR-15 and a shitload of ammo
fire the first bursts in what you know
from your buzzing brain right down to your tingling toes
will be *the* war to save your threatened race from utter extinction
a distinction that sends you blazing away in the local Walmart
courageously mowing down the enemy
school kids and soccer moms, doting grandparents and workaday dads

all in various shades of brown
expecting that *this* statement will certainly rally the troops to fight,
galvanize an army of simple-minded patriots like yourself
to take up arms and stand their ground
liberating one big-box retailer after another
until this once-great country is yours again
and your name is renowned far and wide
as a true hero of the tribe.
But nothing happens like you expected
except you're dead or caught and tried
either way you're buried in one dark hole or another
your life effectively over
your name cursed if mentioned ever
except maybe by some of the basement brethren who blog and tweet like
    you
but never mind, that's not the kind of fame you imagined.
Do you spend the time that passes
all that time moving slower than the drive-thru line
when the computerized check-out crashes
and every minute seems ten sitting there
choking on exhaust and burning good gas —
do you sit in your cell on your ass
with your buddies or alone
not that it matters, not that anything matters *now*
wondering, *WTF was I thinking?*

Just asking.

I Sing of Donald

after e. e. cummings' "i sing of Olaf glad and big"

i sing of Donald (Olaf not)
whose twisted tongue defiles truth:
a prevaricat-or? *yes*, forsooth!

his craven mini-minion-men (squat
snarfing every boastful tweet)
exalt dear Donald's doofus rants;
but — though confronted with his lies
(and dazzled by his falsest teeth) bask
beneath his crooked smile
to bathe in hate he radiates
like a sun whose heat incinerates
makes ash of what was green and sweet;
his kindred kind in congress bent
wary of his tweeting thumbs
(those many least ways not struck dumb)
evoke allegiance in loud and long
encomiums of effusive praise
while Donald (being to all intents
a graven god by self decree
absolves himself of low deceit)
remarks to those who supplicate
"there is more shit you'll gladly eat"

as presidential prerogatives
assert perfection with every call
he calls for those who remonstrate
his excesses both big and small,
"those sonsofbitches all must fall"

Christ! (a trumped redundancy
for those who worship myth and man)
some pray to see his high ascension;

while those of us in condescension
recognize what is must most true:
this mountebank of pus made flesh
is less brave than me:more bronze than you.

Sailing to Mar-a-lago
with all due apologies to William Butler Yeats

I

That is no resort for young men. The old
With new electric carts, golf clubs and bags,
— Those dying dreams of glory — cheaply sold,
In pastel shirts and slacks, designer tags,
Shoes, belts, and caps, boisterous and bold;
Their wealth and privilege, white as any flag,
Snapping in the breeze of their neglect,
Build monuments to what their age respects.

II

This bronzed man is but a vulgar thing,
His belly soft and stuffed into his pants.
He fiddles with his watch and pinkie ring
And plays at being Lord of every dance;
For people do not matter, but they sing
In chorus to his own magnificence;
And therefore he will sail the seas to go
Retire to his home at Mar-a-Lago.

III

O pundits musing of his passing fame,
Recount the many crimes he did commit.
Come to call him out by every name —
Fraud, Liar, Thief, Scoundrel, trumped-up Twit —
To lance the boil and purify with flame
The sickness at the core of all of it:
The lies we tell ourselves to sleep at night,
That only *we* are wholly in God's light.

IV

Once he has left and quit this mortal coil,
His lumpen body politic at rest
Moldering next to him in toxic soil
Gouged from the earth as from his mother's breast,

The young must stand against those who despoil
The promise of this country at its best.
Spurn the Kings and Queens of Mar-a-Lago,
the lies they live, and love, and only know.

An Open Poem
to Senator Ronald Johnson

Anybody can write an email,
or even better, an actual letter;
I've written you many myself,
many I'm guessing you've never read,
that never made it past the poor
intern/s assigned to handle your interactions
with those factions of the public
who constitute your constituency
and feel compelled to write.
Am I right?

I've never received more from you
than a token response, an auto-generated
invitation to subscribe to your monthly
newsletter (along with the occasional
request for quick campaign cash) in which all things
Johnson in the wicked world of Washington
are described for us rubes back home:

Ron standing bravely (alone)
on the Senate floor defending
the privileged few who feel ignored;
Ron holding the door (open)
for the insurrectionists who feel vexatious
about having their votes counted
only once; Ron at the border (closed)
looking gravely concerned at the hordes
of unaccompanied children crashing
our shores with their foreign ways,
carrying with them their foreign malaise
of dope and hope for better days.

Senator, your newsletter is better
than TV. It's like a postcard from a relative
I never see, all about you, saying
Hey, look at me! Don't I look fit?
Don't I look grand? Don't you wish you were

here, next to me where I stand?
Oh, if only!

    That's why I thought I would write
you a poem. A man of your stature deserves
the rapture a poem can bestow — in words
that fly like birds on high, from the snowy
caps of Kilimanjaro atop your furrowed brow,
to the Allen Edmonds cap-toe oxfords
that hold you steadfast to the ground.
Only poetry can capture your lean and lithe
Wisconsin frame, the way it cuts
a commanding figure whatever you wear,
be it jeans and a button-down, open at the neck,
sleeves rolled to the elbow as if to say
Here's one politico unafraid of a little work;
or a tailored three-piece bespoke suit
that exudes the sophisticated elegance
of a self-made man among jerks,
accentuating the moves of a jungle cat
confident in his single-minded pursuit.

    The Ron Johnson of this poem is mythic —
a construct supple as a Shakespearean sonnet,
humble as a Pope couplet, worthy of a Homeric epic.
He is immense in ways only trope can convey,
measurable maybe in iambs of metric feet
rather than the inches of ordinary men, knowable
perhaps in the conceits of metaphor and simile.
He is a Ronald emblematic of his name,
a ruler of counsel greater even than a Donald;
a Johnson more than his essential Johnson-ness
might relate (not that one Johnson isn't the equal
of any other, a bedrock tenet of his
egalitarian beliefs).

    Senator, let this poem be the first brick
in the monument history will build in your
name, an edifice so straight and tall and imposing
future generations will gaze upon it in awe
and exclaim, *Now there's a Johnson!*

Chauvin Shrugged

Chaos is the natural order of things,
apparently; the world has kept spinning on its axis
thanks to the slender shoulders of an Atlas in blue
whose knee on the neck of a black man in Minnesota
was all that kept things as they are
the way that they were for as long as we can remember.

Blandishments beside the point at this point,
with video evidence gone viral
sucking the oxygen out of every argument to the contrary:
what happened on the mean streets
of Minneapolis of all places was necessary
to protect the interests of Those whose whitest intentions
to maintain law and order for all could excuse
a few lapses of judgment by Their boys in blue,
greasing the wheels of justice for the commerce
prosperity and general welfare of Those
who take Their privilege as godly given
and want a slice of everything else from everybody else too.

When Chauvin shrugged
away pleas of "i can't breathe"
taking a knee for the status Quo
so that the Quo could maintain the status They were accustomed to,
the world held its breath and backs bucked
as knees buckled, and the curtain that hid the tiny men
pulling the levers was suddenly ripped aside
for all to see: The grinding machinery behind the machine
that maintained the order we knew
wasn't order at all, but a manufactured kind of spiritual chaos
too corrupt and crippling to keep.

After the Day After

The day after the election but before anybody knew for certain
the sun without our nervous trepidation peeked
over the edge of the horizon and, sensing the scene
much as she had left it, commenced her daily stroll
across the sky. Birds awakened too without much need to know
except that the air was a few degrees warmer
and the wind a knot or two fresher. The millet, flax and thistle
in the feeder in the ceder was still there waiting as it was
the day before, and the world that they expected
was much what they knew and boisterous they flew into it.

The day after the election but before anybody knew for certain
the maple in the front yard waved farewell to more of its leaves
in that stiffened southwesterly breeze. They fell like confetti
around the yard signs that swayed on spindly wire legs
as if preparing to parade, but since nothing was yet decided
and they had nowhere else to go, they stayed to pledge allegiance
to any passersby who still cared to notice.

The day after the election but before anybody knew for certain
the coffee still steamed, the refrigerator still hummed,
the furnace kicked on, and the dog grumbled to be fed.
A garbage truck moved in starts down one side of the street
collecting trash in intermittent stops, the pneumatic whine
of its side-loader arm lifting and lowering in a syncopation
that made the morning methodically mundane. *Everything,*
it seemed to sing, *is what it was, the same. Whatever was promised*
yesterday is for tomorrow to remake and name.

The day after the election that was all anybody knew for certain.

It's a Dog's Life, After All

Sometimes I think
    walking the dog
        watching him snuffle
                snout to the ground
                searching out places
        circling around
    for just the right spot
        to christen the earth
    doing what he does
    so freely from birth
that I have it backwards
                    (or sideways or bent)
this life that I've lived
    this time that I've spent
        worrying minutes
        into hours and days
                of what it all means
                the modern malaise
    of credits and debits
    and 401k's
    political power
    judicial review
    pandemic survival
                (that last one is new)
systemic racism
sanctity of life
antifa fascism
    domestic strife
    deficit spending
        the national debt
        melting ice caps
    frozen assets
    corporate welfare
intelligent design
wealth inequality
                (what's yours is mine)
Black Lives Matter
Blue Ones, too
All Lives Matter

none of them do
      mail-in ballots
      voter suppression
      election fatigue
   election depression
cognitive dissonance
internet trolls
Q-anon shaman
         (a self-written role)
There's too much Everything
and not enough me
   I envy you, friend,
   your freedom to be
      to accept the world
      without judgment or fear
  to follow your nose
from somewhere   to here
   to savor old paths
   as if they were new
      to pretend that you listen
        (when I talk to you)
   Maybe it's backwards
   these rules that we've set
you are the master
and I am the pet
   I'm the one needing
   this walk in the park
      this routine respite
      each day before dark
You're the one leading
directing me home
   to a spot on the sofa
I call my own.

Heresy

I have my doubts
about God
but the Devil makes sense
to me — not
in the comic book way
of red scales
sulfurous breath
serpent's tongue
and barbed tail — no:
that's not the Devil
I see.

The Devil I see
the one I can believe
in is man-
made hate incarnate
seductive as a poem
soft as a psalm
sung in cathedrals
carried in hearts
cultivated in minds
shared in children
blessed in kind.

This Devil gives his
True-believers purpose
something to do
to fill the void
keep their idle
hands busy
with his wicked work
divesting hope
scheming division
investing misery
death and derision
through the long days
and longer nights
of waiting
waiting for God
to finally show
an interest.

Confabulations in COVID Confinement

Confabulating with Myself
During a Pandemic

This is what happens when memory takes a hike with Whitman,
when Williams uses a speculum on your synapses:
You remember moments of poems that free-form float
from trope to trope and stanza to stanza, rearranging themselves
into a phantasmagoria of Frankenverse cobbled together
from pieces of poesy stitched with whimsy.

You sing the body electric with a red wheelbarrow for accompaniment.
You walk with Prufrock through any pretty how town along the trail.
When you come to a hazel wood where two roads might diverge, you
    stop
and wait for the bus to take you to Coney Island.
There, you will be lured by painted women under gas lamps,
but if the light is dying, as it must, all you can do is rage against time.

I recite the best lines of my generation, but I am wracked by envy
for all that came before me, starving and hysterically naked.
I want to peek behind the hemlocks standing hip to hip
to glimpse the secret stuff that I am sure is hidden from me,
but what I find are words, only words, scattered like so many
fallen leaves at my feet, trembling at the approach of the rake.

This is what happens when memory takes a hike with Whitman,
when Williams pries apart your synapses: you digress
and search vainly for egress, any kind of egress you can find.
When you leave you're left right where you began
just to begin again confabulating with yourself,
searching for reasons in the rhymes that come to mind.

Coronavirus Comes a-Calling

Through a microscope it looks like Spring,
a speck of pollen on a bumble bee's wing;
round and erupting with bursts of red,
it could be a blossom in a flower bed.

It floats in droplets of a mist in the air
and falls like the rain seemingly everywhere,
finding purchase on surface or skin,
waiting its moment to worm its way in.

Once in the blood it hides in plain sight
and affixes itself with malicious delight
to the cells of its host, like a creepy house guest
who won't be denied a fortnight's long rest.

Inside it decides to impose its own will:
capricious and cruel, it might cosset or kill,
might fan a fever or conjure a cough —
or it might get mean and really play rough.

Satisfied or spent (who's really to say?),
it will pack up and leave, call it a day,
as mysteriously as it made its arrival,
leaving millions behind in a fight for survival.

The Covid-19, like its fellow diseases,
strikes where it wants and takes whom it pleases.
Its warning is simple for us small-minded men:
Like the seasons I come, again and again.

Everything's Virtual

What was isn't anymore,
stopped like a clock by something infinitesimally small,
a mitochondrial glitch in the gears
that has changed virtually everything overnight.
Gone are the verities we once knew:
the crowning of champions in crowded arenas,
the throngs that belong cheering Opening Day,
shopping malls and concert halls,
the surge of passengers boarding a train,
the conga line of travelers exiting a plane.
Where once we happily squeezed together to include one more,
now we distance ourselves from neighbors
behind the security of closed doors,
avoiding contagion in isolation,
finding safety in quarantine.

Virtual life has gone viral in algorithms and apps:
virtual school, virtual commencements,
virtual reunions, virtual church,
virtual weddings, virtual wakes.
We Zoom through days sheltering in place
in virtual rooms of face time
in virtual certainty that tomorrow will be virtually the same
as today, part of a string of days
that loop into weeks without tying
virtually anything together.

We are a species unique unto ourselves.
We prize the clarity of beginnings,
the certainty of endings.
We bank on the investment
that things start and stop on schedule.
What comes between,
the meaning of the middle,
is a means to an end of a job
that leads inevitably to another and the next after that,
a succession of tasks that makes sense in the order
of things because that is the way things are ordered
in the finite world we have fashioned for ourselves.

Most of us aren't emotionally conditioned to survive
the Infinite Middle in which we find ourselves caught,
a virtual Hell that virtually repeats itself over and over,
like a piece of muzak droning in an elevator
stuck between floors that never stops.

Cooling My Cockles
in COVID Confinement

There's nothing like a hot cockle
to get one through the tempests of time
these days of peril and pandemic present.
Even lukewarm cockles can sometimes suffice,
suffusing the soul with a rosy glow
comforting as the blush of embarrassment
one gets from a surprising compliment
or unexpected kiss;

but cockles left exposed,
naked and abandoned to the whims
of this mercurial world, or worse — chilling
unceremoniously like a tinge of tea
left at the bottom of the cup
as Covid curdles the milk of commerce
with a ruthlessness of a robber baron
of old — that's cold!

My cockles scream
for kindness and care,
the kind that comes quite naturally
with human intercourse and communal cheer;
but locked away in confinement,
leery of every unmasked smile
that veers too close, wary of every snuffle
and snort of benign bonhomie,
they freeze with fear and recoil.

Winter is coming, but my cockles don't care.
They are already there, encrusted in ice.
Thanksgiving, Christmas, New Year's to come
and my cockles turn a cold shoulder.
They're numb. Wake them, they say,
when things again are nice
and a cockle can warm the heart once more
like a draft of spirits and spice.

Consult a Medical Professional First

My doctor was dubious, indubitably so:
Regeneron, maybe; *Hydroxychloroquine*, no.
A cocktail of steroids, boosters and bromides
(injected, ingested, imbibed, or applied)
was still being tested in clinical trials,
and a vaccine could take more than a while;
so who knows if and when, there's just no guarantee,
but what I was proposing was nuts as can be!

> Combating the Covid, the scourge of our time,
> with nothing but poesy, meter and rhyme?
> A diet of dactyls, iambs and anapests,
> served in a salad of ballads and sonnets,
> sprinkled with simile and an allusion or two,
> was a recipe for disaster too literal to be true!
> Was I offering myself as experimental specimen?
> Had I considered the side effects of such radical regimen?
> The shortness of breadth that comes with haiku?
> The pedantics of epics — loggorhea, too?
> Not to mention dissonance or irony deficiency,
> loose vowel assonance or abstruse metonymy,
> antanaclasis or hyper hyperbole,
> metaphorical catachreis or obtuse synechdoche?

I sat there chastened, in my underwear and socks,
as he checked my reflexes and listened to my heart,
measured my pressures and scribbled in his file,
then considered a moment that ended with a smile.
Covid's not something to sneeze at, he said,
and your work — well, the little *I've* read —
hardly qualifies as legitimate verse.
Listen to your doctor: Don't make things worse.

Dark Matters

I read recently astronomers have created a telescope
powerful enough to peer through the black spaces
of the universe. They hope to gather more than a glimpse
of our creation at the edge of an expanse,
ever expanding, they explain (*in language
at least as dense as the directions for this toy
I am attempting to assemble for my granddaughter
on her birthday*) to prove the simple supposition
that life is no fluke. We exist as a binomial certainty,
replicated within certain discrete variations, of course,
with a contrapositive redundancy factor
that can be mathematically calculated.

I find this oddly reassuring.
It explains, I suppose, the feeling I sometimes get
that there is another Me somewhere hidden
in the dark matters of my mind, orbiting me
from a privileged perspective. This other Me mimics
my moods and mannerisms (*with motives
murky as the gap between Steps 2 and 3
in piecing the proper parts together to get to 4
on the instructions included in the packaging*).
It is my anti-Self, in perpetual apposition
to my postulate Self, there to give each expression
its equal and opposite due, every action inherent
in an alternative outcome.

The idea should be cause for celebration for middling poets
(*and toy assemblers*) everywhere, but I must confess
to being of two minds about the matter.

On one hand, I should be ecstatic:
No longer need I fear failure in the harsh light
of reality, for somewhere on the flip side,
in the depthless darkness of non-reality,
I'm a success! My stuff makes sense (*assembled*)
and might even sell!

On the other hand, my hermeneutics won't let me

off the hook so easily. It tells me in no uncertain
catholic terms that light is harsh for a purpose —
to expose the faults in our fallible souls and illuminate
a critical Truth: There's a reason some things don't sell,
even in the pulsating variables of expanding galaxies
where you'd think anything might sell . . .
(and a reason why two mismatched screws
and a flange still lay before me on the table, unused).

I suppose astronomers will continue to probe the heavens
overhead, building bigger and better telescopes
to chase dark energy to its source, but I would appreciate
an alternative device: an equally powerful microscope
that could peer imperviously into the dark matter of my mind
in search of an intelligence that might explain the mess I've made
of (*this toy*) this poem.

Mugged on Christmas Eve

I was careful.
I scrupulously avoided the worst places
(churches, schools)
and confined myself to copious spaces
(outdoor malls, cavernous halls)
thinking I could fool with fate.
I even took the shot
(early this year, but, alas, too late)
and practiced hygiene
like a germaphobe on a bender,
scrubbing my hands pink
after every casual encounter.
I cornered the market on anti-bacterial gel
and was up to my nostrils in essential oils.
I gargled mornings.
I neti-potted afternoons.
I vaporized my evenings
and fantasized fecklessly
this year could be different:
The alphabet of influenza
that had plagued me seasons past
would at last leave *me* unspelled;
but such cocky conceit,
I should have known,
can never go unpunished long.
Every Christmas gives a cold . . .

. . . and so it was on Christmas Eve,
when my chestnuts should have been roasting
in open fires for tiny tots with cheeks aglow —
when I could have been caroling
on lamp-lit corners and making merry memories
of jingling bells and sleigh rides
through a Hallmark world of woods and snow —
my throat turned red as Rudolph's nose
and I started barking like an agitated reindeer.
What my body produced from the depths
of my being decorum decrees
must remain undescribed.

The only Christmas spirits I wanted to see
came from a bottle, served in a tumbler,
with honey and lemon and warm ginger beer . . .

. . . a week later, when I crawled out of bed
to welcome a New Year that looked
regrettably gray as the old, I was a chastened man
who (like Scrooge) had learned a lesson:
A person can live his life meanly and small
or grandly and large, miserly and bitter
or prodigal and sweet; he can take more
precautions than money can buy
or a pharmacist entreat;
he can even, perhaps, in the fullness
of his folly convince himself he is nigh
impervious to the perils of this world . . .

But beware:

All it takes is the "influence of the stars"
to bring him crashing to earth — one tiny microbe,
mugging him on Monday,
knocking his ass into next week — to prove
the point: there's no escaping
the flu.

COVID Copy

for the doubters and deniers

What if the calendar caught itself the Covid too,
came down with the jitters that jumbled its months,
let May mix with March and August piggyback April
all the way through summer into spring,
so there was no end to things and things
went on again until again began again
without knowing when to end
because there was no end to begin with
and everything was just the middle stuck
like a fault in a record groove that won't move
playing the same chord over and over?

What if days no longer mattered,
Sun and Sat and Mon and Fri
can Tues and Thurs all they want
because there was no Wednes anymore
to balance the week, no tipping point
to teeter on and totter into the weekend
because there is no weekend to look forward to,
just another morning following evening
with an afternoon in between
of time taking its time to get there
even though there was nowhere to go
and nothing left when you arrive?

What if hours quit being hours
and collapsed into minutes, and what if minutes
hacked themselves into moments
that stopped and started in syncopation
with a ventilator, breathing in and out
the seconds that beg for thirds and fourths
as the body unravels itself from
the world and marks time waiting
while the virus attacks the lifespan
of all of us until all of us is whittled away
to none and none of us is all that is left
to copy what we've become?

Would Covid get your attention then?

New Year 2021

There were 31,622,400 seconds in 2020,
the year just past. Trust me, I've done the math,
but you can Google it yourself if you're a skeptic.
Those 31,622,400 seconds filled 527,040 minutes,
8,784 hours, or 366 days if you'd rather. Like billions
of others on this planet I stumbled or staggered
through them all, survived the cycle of diseases
both foreign and domestic that took the lives of millions,
avoided war and violence that killed hundreds of thousands
more across the globe, rose each morning
to claim whatever part of the earth was mine
to subsist, unlike thousands of others hourly who ceased
to exist. They fell through cracks in time
to another side of the human experience,
to manifest the blankness or glimpse the divine,
however you choose to measure the meaning
of what it is to be alive.

Of those 31,622,400 seconds, the one that people
anticipated the most was the last, the 31,622,400[th]
that made the leap to the first of year 2021. Fireworks
lit darkened skies, glitzy balls dropped down poles;
corks popped, music swirled, people sang, wine spilled
for those who stayed up late as it took to take it all in,
to kiss or clasp, wish or grasp someone else, maybe
a complete stranger, masked or not, socially distant
or intimately close, in a traditional New Year's greeting
before joining in a chorus of "Auld Lang Syne"
without having any real understanding of what the words
Robert Burns wrote actually mean. Did it matter
if old acquaintance be forgot and never brought to mind?

Twenty-twenty — the year of Covid, of collapse,
of climate-driven catastrophes, of racial unrest,
of political protest, of partisan divides — was over
and past; and even though that first breath of the new
didn't seem so different from the last gasp of the old,
there was promise that this time our resolutions
to change for the better would be kept. After all,

we have 31,535,999 seconds, or 525,600 minutes,
or 8,760 hours, or 365 days left to get something done.
Trust me, I've done the math.

The United States of Time

Is time a line flat as Florida
following a flow that inevitably drops us all
in a Gulf into which we disappear,
in depths swept clean by streams
that deposit our souls on some distant shore?
Or is time a range rocky as Colorado
looming before us, an impervious horizon,
imposing in its saw-toothed peaks,
defying us to scale its trails to dizzying heights
from which to glimpse an other side
where hidden vistas are revealed?

The more time I've wasted wondering
from one state of anxiety to another
of anticipation, the less it seems I have
to show for what I've accomplished.
I'm a tourist in my own life desperate
for a map to give me some direction —
or maybe a brochure of highlights
that I can keep as a souvenir
of all the minutes, months, and years
I've spent searching for myself
without success.

It's hard to draw a sensible line
through the mess I've made
of my meanderings, from the swamps
of my lowlands to the buttes of my highs.
My Louisiana's are sometimes indistinguishable
from the Montana's in my memory bank,
but that hasn't stopped me from writing
checks against my account. It's the price
we pay for wandering day to day
until we tap out. Me,

I intend to borrow until I'm broke,
time permitting: I'll keep putting one foot
in front of the other cross-country, downwind,
in-county and transcendental until I'm bootless

and bankrupt, looking for something
I won't know until it finds me.

We're Allowed to Grieve for Little Things Still

The minutes lost, the memories lapsed
that vanish like effervescence in the glass bowl
life has become these days, I lament

the friendships paused, the trips postponed
as one morning becomes another afternoon
in a week that dissolves into months, I mourn

the parties forfeit, the meetings zoomed
in the crawl of conversation digitally buffered
through logarithms of coded love, I regret

all I can offer in this year of immense misery
circling the globe like malignant electrons
is this little thing of words to share in grief.

Shouldering On

I slipped on ice three Saturdays back
crossing the street at the corner
(poetic justice adjudicated
for this inveterate jaywalker)
and came down hard on my right shoulder.

That shoulder has shouldered
its share of this world for 67 years
without comment, but now I lift it
or rotate and shift it, it crackles
and pops like breakfast cereal
and barks back at me in the moment.

I've iced it and massaged it,
kneaded it and heated it
and popped Advil at night to forget it,
figuring the next morning might
make things just as they were
four Fridays back, but no.

My wife says, *See a doctor*
and I suppose I might maybe,
but I can imagine him poking
and prodding and telling me,
You should have come in sooner
as he studies a few snapshots
of said shoulder and shows me
what the world has done to me
and what he recommends to fix it.

That's why I am loath to go,
wary that the cure will be as hard
as the world was to me
that moment three Saturdays ago
when it met me without an inch of give.

The lessons I've learned are simple:
You fall, you get up.
You take your lumps and live.

Saturday Spring 2021

This year the calendar says Saturday
Spring will poke its nose from the muddy mess of March
to see itself reflected in a sky brilliantly blue,
to wash itself in warmth that might make August shiver
but today is a promise of things to come
finally for wintry Wisconsin
after a year of Covid confusion and confinement.

What matters most to those of us who have endured
isn't that the sudden swing from grueling-gray?
and bracing-bitter to tee-shirt temperatures
and enfolding sun signifies a definitive end
to our ordeals. There will be turbulence and torment still
in the days and weeks to come, we know,
and patience will be tested by the moody turns
of April and the fickle whims of May,

who sometimes treat us with the casual cruelty
of sisters. A day such as this, though, one
sweetly dissolving on the tongues of all
of us, old and young, is reward for our resolve
to have kept faith through those many days
we were denied the weekends we remember
with families and friends from a time
we took for granted — candy of a kind
that can sustain us, keep us savoring until more.

Uncertain Spring 2020

Don't blink peering out
windows, you might miss
it: that stray shaft of sunlight
slicing through clouds —
it lifts the green from doubt
if just for a minute
in a lawn still broodingly brown.

April wants to keep seasonal
distance from her winter
relatives February and March;
but her days can carry
only so much hope
and she's so uncertain
what to do next,
there is so much to do.

Outside looking in
in this time of viral gloom
she sees rooms in need of airing;
senses your impatience, too,
for more than a slice of sun,
more than a breath of breeze,
to lift you from the doubt
of these uncertain days.

She coaxes a green shoot
from the detritus of your window box;
seduces a bird on a branch
to suddenly sing:
Little gifts to reassure you —
there is still magic
in the making.
Be patient.
It's just Spring.

I Find Myself Now in the Most Usual Places

From the window of a car, a bus, or a train
I glimpse myself masked among the many I see,
zipping past storefronts or houses — stepping, stopping,
grouping at intersections waiting for a light to change.
I have to give a second look, maybe a third,
the sudden recognition seems so strange to me.
I wonder, *What am I doing over there instead of here?*
Why am I wearing that coat? Where did I get that cap?
When did I start wearing those glasses?

I always seem involved in something —
a conversation, a conspiracy, a concerted effort
to get someplace other than where I am —
and sometimes the moment passes after
I think things through. I realize, *That isn't me!*
What was I thinking? I would be more socially distant,
standing off to the side, avoiding eye contact. I would be reading
clouds, not faces. I would be listening
for the cracks in the sidewalk to crack somebody up.

I wouldn't be sitting on a step stoop, maskless,
cradling a cold beer, relaxing. No,
I'd be throwing my head back far as I could,
mind open wide, wondering
how much of this new world
can a fella swallow before he drowns
and drifts away somewhere else?

Interior Life, One Year in Pandemic

From inside
the prison of my mind
corners are a comfort in confinement.
They suggest an orderly sense of direction,
of safety in circumspection
for a body stuck in the middle of things
fearing there is no way out.
A corner too is a confluence of certainty
and doubt, a collision of geometric planes
that both constrains but contains
disruption of a line that suddenly ends
then begins again,
like the road outside my house
where an intersection can be a promise
of choice and change.

One year in
behind walls and windows
separating me from the wider world
of disease and infection, I am reduced
to routine and introspection.
I swim from room to room
with restless anticipation,
contemplating what corners can be safely cut
to hasten my eventual emancipation.
How and when will I emerge again
from an interior life of waiting,
to suddenly burst forth with wings
like the mayfly, to live so fully
within my community
a day isn't fleeting but a lifetime?

COVID is a cruel teacher, its lessons
succinct and clear: Embrace what you have
while you have it, love without fear
because anything and everything
can end in a second,
extend to a year.

The Life Lessons in Leftovers

They languish in the cold and dark
some in Ziploc bags or saran-wrapped plates,
others carry-out boxed or Tupperware bowled,
leftovers that guilt dictates be kept,
too good or too much to throw away.

You paid to have them made-to-order
or picked them up on the go
or took the time to DIY them
for family, friends or yourself;
but Mother told you, Father warned you
eyes can be bigger than appetites sometimes
so much of what would be otherwise wasted
can be prudently stored for some other time.

Those waste-not / want-not lessons of childhood
there somewhere in the Frigidaire
pushed to the back of cluttered shelves
behind cartons of juice and bottles of beer,
are reminders of just how temporal things are

. . . until that time when time determines
what's been left has over-stayed,
its shelf-life long since lapsed
and whatever pleasure you imagined
reheating and eating that portion you saved
has been replaced by something new,
something fresher, something you're sure
will nourish tomorrow as you feed yesterday
into the disposal to make some room
today. It's a lesson learned from life's repast:
Savor the savory in the moment
because what's left over doesn't last.

The Five Stages of Hair Loss

A mid-March snow has me reminiscing about my hair:
A spattering too sparse to really matter,
it lets the grass poke through in patches
in a pattern that I see every morning in the mirror
staring back and mocking me. The desert of my scalp,
a sloping dune between oases, was once a fertile field
rolling free from ear to ear. The locks that gave me cover,
long and lustrous, falling easy, started leaving in my 40s,
growing thinner year by year. First I felt denial:
What I'm seeing can't be true! It's some natural phenomena,
like what happens with caribou. They migrate for awhile,
and some might fail to return; but the herd seems always
just as thick with young ones newly born. Then anger
raised its raging face, both furious and frantic,
placing blame where it belongs — on parents and genetics.
Or maybe it's pollution, all those toxins in the air,
responsible for killing the healthy follicles of my hair!
My anger eased, as anger must; I began to reason out
a treatment plan guaranteed to succeed scientifically,
without doubt: I would massage my scalp
with oils every morning, noon and night, replenishing
vital nutrients that I'd starved into full flight.
And I'd eat only those kinds of food that hair needs
best to grow, and supplement my diet with multiple
vitamins, row by row. Yet the harder it seemed I oiled,
the more hair I seemed to lose, so I replaced my fancy diet
and expensive pills with cheaper booze. *If I'm going bald*
let me get there lifted from this funk — happy, free from worry,
feeling cocky and reeling drunk! But drinking only made
things worse, as drinking often will; those bloodshot
eyes could clearly see my hair was thinning still.
It took me time to get here to this place where I accept
that the head I carry with me will stay nakedly bereft.
My hirsute days are history, a figment of my past,
evident now in photographs and memories while they last.
I rarely think of what I had once growing on my dome;
and while mid-March snows might cruelly jest, might mock
me now my hairy chest is hairier than my dwindling crest,

I'm content to let things rest: My mornings are free from
the tangled mess of blow-dryers, brushes and styling stress.
I don't even own a comb!

Everything Empties and Refills

The world outside my window is white
in ways that seem ethereal and brittle;
the temperature these past few days
has hovered in that limbo between
frost and thaw, conjuring ghostly fog
that powders the trees and bushes
in the early dawn gray with a white
rime delicate as dust. Morning minutes
suspend themselves like caught breath
waiting for the sun to bring some color
back to things, but in this instant
everything empties into a white
that whispers of inevitability,
of relinquishment,
of sleep so deep
the dreams we dream are draining —
until that first sliver of light cuts through
cloud and the day refills like the cup
in my hand and I sip.

Topsy-turvy Time

Don't give me antsy-pantsy
crinkum-crankum clickety-clack,
fluffy-ruffle dillydally
froufrou flickety-flack,
hoity-toity pish posh
house mouse bumpety-bump
or chiffchaff chuck-a-luck
hobnob plunkety-plunk;

I want hootchy-kootchy razzmatazz
yum-yum knockety-knock,
hotsy-totsy fizgig
hickory dickory dock,
no hugger mugger fuddy duddy
tut-tut flip-flop smack —
just the wild tuzzy-muzzy
holus-bolus crackerjack!

Rummaging Through a Rack of Rumination

Bisextile Curious MWM Seeking Answers

bisextile (adj.) noting the extra day in a leap year

Every four years I wonder what it would be like
to be bisextile, squeezed into this world
between February and March, born
on that astronomical oddity of a quadrennial day.
To be openly, proudly, unabashedly bisextile
in a world dictated by the Gregorian chance
of a heterogeneous calendar!
How special would that make me?
The notion fires my imagination to lunar heights:
it gets me thinking how ordinary my life is
being simply *sextile,* compared to what if.

Could I nominally disappear
until every fourth year, an entity whose birthday
was nothing but an intercalary abnormality
concocted by mathematical calculation?
Would I be free to choose and sample
months in tandem, my moods a fluctuation
taking me from austere February
to mercurial March on a whimsy of days
with the most significant one missing
three-quarters of the time, there only in anticipation?
And what of drivers' licenses, draft lottery
obligations, school registrations, social security
administrations, and a host of other matters
the straight calendar crowd takes for granted?
Where would I, a blameless bisextilist adrift
in such society, fit in?

The world throws a lot at us at birth:
We're expected to measure up to *something*
useful and unique, extending in an unbroken line
from a date certified on the first legal document
we're given with our names affixed.
We carry that burden with us until we depart,
at which point our accumulation of days is judged

as being worthwhile or a waste.
My bisextile fantasies are sadly simply that,
borne from a need to make haste — now
I am sixty-seven and daily accruing further evidence
that the life I have lived to this point is proof:
The things I can be accused of accomplishing of note
are only those things noted daily in the doing.

Drinks with Peckinpah: An Imaginary Tome of Momentary Significance

He was sitting on his haunches,
knees up, slouched against a stucco wall of Old Mexico, a restaurant
on the south corner of True West mall out past the interchange
     connecting
the old highway with the new interstate spur in this suburban community
     sprawl
gnawing the edges of once pristine desert.

He was wearing faded jeans, thin at the knees, brown huaraches gray
with dust and chalk, and a four-pocket embroidered guayabera shirt
that had once been the color of clay, sun-bleached now to a color so pale
     it looked cirrhotic.
A multi-colored bandanna wrapped his head and black sunglasses, of
     course,
hid his eyes, but I could tell he was looking at me as I crossed an asphalt
     parking lot
punctuated in clusters with cars and pickups arranged so as to look
     haphazard.

I'd just left a multi-screen theater presenting a retrospective of three of
     his films, shown
in what was called the "Artisan House," a trendy idea to squeeze some
     revenue
from the smallest venue, with capacity for fifty people who wanted
     something more
than the latest Marvel Universe extravaganza and would pay ten dollars
     for the privilege.
Less than a hundred bucks worth of audience had just finished the mid-
     afternoon matinee
of *The Wild Bunch,* but I was the last out of the auditorium
because I'd waited for the credits to drop and the house lights to lift
     before leaving.

Canned mariachi music spilled from speakers into the parking lot,

floating on the spicy smells of grilling meat and sizzling oil pumped from
    the kitchen exhausts.
His head shifted almost imperceptibly with my approach
and his hands, which had been busy playing with a length of string, froze
when I did doing a double-take.
For a man dead since 1984 he looked pretty damn good.
I stood there stiller than Lot's wife, staring.
This he seemed to find amusing.
Whadja think?   he asked abruptly
Worth the pain?

That got me.
Not what I thought a ghost would say,
not that I've ever spoken to a ghost before,
let alone the ghost of a man who had thoroughly haunted my
    imagination
when he was alive and kicking up a fuss, endlessly rewriting his
    reputation.
I worked my tongue around an answer that didn't sound like a
    prevarication.
"What can I say? It's your legacy, Sam.
There's no escaping a legacy, is there?"

That got *him*.
A corner of his mouth twitched in a smile.
He zoomed in on me suddenly like he was one of the cumbersome
    Panavision cameras
he'd lugged across Mexico in 1968, really taking me in.
That legacy worth a drink? he said angling.
My afterlife is hell.
I'm drier than your granddaddy's scalp.

"Why not?" I said.
I thought about massaging the line with my best Warren Oates
but reconsidered and helped him to his feet instead.
He brushed dirt and debris from the back of his pants and followed me
    into the restaurant,
a typical suburban eatery, a big dining area of tables and booths
separated from a sit-down bar by a half-wall, festooned with overgrown
    plants, waxy green.
Everything was bright and vulgar with a polished sheen; a mural
depicting three Mexican peons, larger than life in big hats and colorful
    serapes

leading a burro through a desert landscape of giant cacti and Chuparosa,
    filled an entire wall.
Maybe half a dozen tables were filled with parties of two, three, or four,
in various stages of being served by a couple of waiters
costumed like they'd stepped right out of the painting on the wall.

A smiling young woman greeted us almost immediately.
A name-tag identified her as Aimee. She was blond and bubbly,
looked like she should have been wearing a cheerleader's uniform
rather than the peasant blouse and flounced skirt her employers had her
    outfitted in.
"Welcome to Old Mexico!" she said, grabbing two laminated menus
the size of window cards.

Jeezus, Sam muttered, taking it all in.
I motioned to the bar and Aimee returned the menus to the rack.
We moved to a couple of stools back from the only other customer
    there,
a salesman by the looks of him, with thinning black hair,
staring at the screen of his cell phone while a frozen margarita in an
    enormous goblet
puddled the bar top in front of him.
The bartender, whose tag read Jose, set down between us
a basket of chips and a divided dish of salsa, one half red and one-half
    green.
"Spicy," he said, pointing at the red;
"not so much," nodding at the green.
I ordered a Modelo, Sam four fingers of Patron *anejo,* no ice.
He sniffed the liquor before drinking. *Nice,* he said and downed half the
    glass in one swallow, then
took his glasses off, letting me see his eyes. Widened,
they looked milky and sallow, like marbles
set in the sockets of a dissolute doll.
Truth is, he said, apropos of nothing. *I was never good with it.*
Change. Things change. People change. I didn't.
Couldn't. That's what killed me. Keeps killing me
every goddamn time somebody shows that goddamn movie and pulls me back.
He put his glasses on, finished his drink, ordered another with a gesture.
Everything I ever did was just some futile attempt to suspend time, freeze a moment.
Don't get me wrong, he paused as the fresh drink was placed in front of him
with a ceremonial flourish by Jose, which Sam acknowledged with a
    smile.
A good barkeep is a true artist, my friend. A real *artist.*

Then he disappeared inside himself for a while before returning.
Don't get me wrong, he repeated, discerning the hole he'd left
in what he was thinking. *My ego's big as the next guys. Maybe bigger.*
I wanted to make the best film ever made every time I made one,
but it was the work that juiced me. The doing. The making!
Once the film was in the can, so was I.

He smiled wider, a kind of wry grin that comes from a moment of
    amused recognition.
There were over thirty-six hundred cuts Lou and I made piecing The Bunch
    together.
Everyone took a piece out of me.
What's that old saying? 'Death by a thousand cuts'?
In my case it was death by three thousand six hundred and forty-three cuts, count 'em.
But what the hell. It was something to do and I'm proud I did it,
'legacy' be damned.

He disappeared inside himself again, staring into his drink as if the gold
    liquor in the glass
had an answer for some question only he knew to ask.
I waited for him to loop around back to me and finally he did.
He drained his drink in one long swallow,
slammed his glass on the bar with a finality that sounded hollow.
Where's the head in this joint? he asked the room.
Jose explained how to find it as Sam slid from his stool.
He made a show of patting his pockets. Grinned a sheepish smile like he
    was
some forgetful old fool, harmless and sweet. *I don't have much need for*
    money, he said.
"No problem," I said.
"My treat."

He took a couple steps out the bar, then stopped, turned back to face me
    full on.
I saw myself reflected in the mirrored lenses of his glasses,
older now by several years than he was when he quit his life but not this
    world.
What he saw was someone maybe resolute, still looking.
Want my advice, friend?
Find something worth killing yourself doing.
Do it the best you know.
That's the only 'legacy' worth leaving.
The only one worth remembering anyhow.

Everything else? . . . is bullshit.
Then he wandered off into Old Mexico
and disappeared into the myth of it.

More Assembly Required

I am a work in progress
much as this poem is.
Even though I've spent years,
decades even, assembling
a self that makes sense,
might even be appealing
in an odd sort of way
to the sensibilities of others,
I find myself oddly at odds
with the pieces I've selected
and placed in composition.

There are no random words,
but every choice is random
and randomly changes the meaning
depending on how it's used.
I try to be intentional,
I strive to be consistent,
but one word out of place
makes everything I seem to be
so accidental and different.

If only people were poems,
the kinds of poems we measure
out in rhythmic feet, with meaning
determined and discrete
in the ends we rhyme
and the lines we break,
we could read each other
for the unique works we are,
revised and complete.

But I'm no poem, I can assure you:
All my pieces are in pieces
and nothing seems to fit.
At my age you'd think
I'd have some of this shit figured
out, at least an idea of what to keep
in, but I'm up to my chin

with words that don't explain,
just obfuscate, and no matter
how I assemble them to show me
I end up dissembling all the more, me.
I can't even punctuate this line right, everything I do runs on wrong at
      length for everyone to see.

A Poetry of Personalia

Wisdom comes through suffering... Aeschuylus

You'd think it would be inverse,
that suffering comes from knowing *too much*.
Look how content cattle are in their fields,
grazing in sublime ignorance. If they knew
for one enlightened moment their fate, to go
from being someone's pastoral memory today
to somebody's cheeseburger tomorrow,
would they welcome such wisdom?
Would that mouthful of grass go down as easy
if they had an inkling?

I've chewed this over for a while, thinking
according to Aeschuylus, I just don't *know* enough
because I haven't *suffered* enough.
The life I've lived thus far is lacking
in the lessons imposed upon those
writers and artists of great renown,
whose back stories are so heavily peppered
with pain their biographies burn like curry
going down. Think Poe, Van Gogh, Wallace and Plath;
El Greco, O'Keefe, Sexton and Munch.
Their lives were packed with so much madness
and struggle, the art they created came to us
shrink-wrapped in wisdom of a kind
you just can't buy.

I know, I've tried. I've searched my soul,
ransacked my history, looking for that wellspring
of suffering I could tap that would yield
an ocean of tears crystallized into great art,
but all I can do is fake it. Face it:
I just don't have the biography to make it.

What you hear from me isn't a tortured wail
of wisdom distilled into blank verse.
It's much more terse: *Moo.*

Love/Sick

To feel too much of this world is a dangerous thing.
Taking in more than is emotionally recommended
can kill a body as ruthlessly as any virus.
Better to hide in the herd, stay
in one's lane perfecting the immunity
of anonymity—be what was born, I was told:
a white middle class American male
of solid suburban sensibilities
striding sensibly into senior citizenship
with a 401(k) portfolio securely tucked under one arm,
specified benefit direct-deposited pension under the other,
certain investments and insurance instruments safely locked away
for the eventuality of that day when the estate becomes probate.

I swallowed that program, Brother. Ended up so constipated
with longing, my call wasn't a yawp, full-throated and barbaric,
but a civilized whimper pungent as a fart.

Look at me:
I am nondescript as a shopping cart,
prolific as a mushroom.
Turn any corner on any street
in any community of middle income means
and you will likely as not see me
and miss me in one glance.
Yet I am here and there wherever
you look, waiting for the cliché
to suddenly become unique,
the fungible to finally become me.

I fell in love with the world too late in life
for romantic consummation
to offer more than manic commiseration.
Time might add texture to the landscape of our lives
but it has no eye for order.
Derangement is its signatory style,
chaos guaranteed. No amount of plotting
is likely to succeed. The more we seek
to impose our own designs on things,

the less we have to show for it;
until the things we valued most,
held to the tightest, are reduced to detritus
and dust in our hands, worth whatever is the going rate
of the dirt it takes to fill a hole.

(In my next life, I'd rather be a mole, just for the thrill
of blindly finding the light at the end of my tunnel.)

I am sick with love, in love with love
in all its manifestations. It seeds within me
in florid germination, the tendrils of its roots
wrapping tightly around my tongue when I try to speak.
It makes me weak. The sounds I make are not words:
They are waves breaking in the vast void of space, an echo
of impulses that ceaselessly swell and recede,
washing over this world that I love
too much to concede.

Someone said, more as an after-thought,
reading the riot of my heart,
You must be a poet. That's not very smart.
Poems should be considered controlled substances.
Ingesting too many too quickly will kill you.

But what else can an addict do?

Self-Portrait, 2019

Born as I was under the sign of Eisenhower
I am of the age when my miles and years collude
to make each new morning a mystery
of suddenly sentient aches
rising to the surface like lunker fish
pressing snouts against watery light;

when the blood that has reliably sustained me
is liable to do something stupid-like,
swim thickly through narrowing veins,
pool in places that slow the flow
to fingers and toes making every touch
an attenuation gumming and numbing
the feel of the familiar until what I clasp
is only what I can see;

and what I see in the vanity mirror
above the sink isn't what I think of me inside,
a vanity that overlooks the gray and sparse
that time has made grayer and sparser,
or the sedentary slouch from too much time
spent curling into couches
and snacking on junk food and trash TV.

Is this really me now I want to ask
that face staring back at me
grizzled and grainy — an image
that my secret self-studies with amused detachment
before withdrawing into the hollows
of a daily consciousness that skims like a stone
across the surface of things, glassy and serene.

I am retired and living the dream
older now than one of my grandfathers was
when he unexpectedly passed:
He could peel an apple with a pen knife
in one unbroken spiral that would jounce
like a spring as he worked his way round
with the concentration of Michelangelo

finding David in the marble;
and when he finished, he would hold that
peel on the palm of one hand before me,
and with the other fold the coils carefully
conjuring an apple empty of itself inside,
then raise his eyebrows puckishly as if to say, *See?*

But I was just a boy then too silly to grasp
the significance of what life meant
dispensed in measures half pleasure and pain,
too quick to snap at every shiny thing
dragged enticingly before me
in a world I cynically saw as just another shell game.
Fuck this I liked to say, poser that I am.
I'll just go with the flow like everybody else.
Get mine while I can.

Life, however, bestows its lessons in unexpected jerks,
setting the hook deepest those times it really hurts.

And sometimes the only way to survive yourself
is to kick hard against the current your bulk has made
in the drift of things — keep kicking
until you find yourself again somewhere upstream.

Koan Poem

More people write poems than read them
so what purpose does it serve to add another
to the list of things piling in plain sight
in this cluttered world? . . . yet here we are
again pondering the paradoxical:
What fool conducts orchestras
with one hand and applauds with the other
when the only audience listening
is a tree fallen in a forest unobserved?

Poems are like prayer flags at the topmost
of mountains only a few of us
have the inclination to climb:
They flutter in the wind, like leaves
strung from the zenith of trees,
beseeching the sky to answer them
beneath the roar of inscrutable silence.

Blind Sides

The everyday has this essential trait: it allows no hold ... It
is the unperceived, first in the sense that one has always
looked past it . . . Maurice Blanchot

I keep looking for things in the wrong place:
I search for art in museums and galleries,
overlooking the saltshaker in my hand
whose utility and design are perfection defined,
staring me in the face. I rummage for poetry
in the pages of books, through volumes slender or thick,
and anthologies that offer a smorgasbord of verse
for every taste from which to pick, ignoring
the poems that sneak up behind me
disguised as flowers, trees, or birds,
that speak in tongues of color that blind me,
in silence too pure for words. I prospect for love
in grand gestures of romance —
golden vistas, orchestrated music,
pastel costumes and choreographed dance —
missing the miracle of minutes
that play out daily like thread from a spool,
stitching together two lives locked by chance
in an embrace so seamless we seem one, not two.

Kobe

You don't need a poem
to tell you how random the world can be.

Things can change in a syllable.

Helicopters fall from the sky unexpectedly
in the time it takes to write a word.

Lives end without punctuation,
without the illusion of continuity.

A poem can look for meaning in the absurd,
might even find epiphany
in the most abrupt of endings,

but words make meager metaphors
when fate interrupts and life rolls randomly
off the rim: your ordered world

caroms crazily away &
that daily delirium of busy banality

stops

suddenly making sense — like
finding a lotus flowering in a puddle
within a crack of broken cement.

An Exemplary Life

It's what we all aspire to, each day
waking to possibility fulfilled, our own
to accomplish in some measure small or large,
walking steadfastly into a life *we* build,
making moments for ourselves that others
will commend as worth the work and while.

Thousands of years before us and thousands
more to come, among billions of lives lived
already and more each morning born,
some impulse implores us to strive to be one
that makes a difference for those who adore us,
and for multitudes of others never known.

For to be exemplary is a most human desire,
regardless of who we might be. It drives
our dreams of what we inspire in ourselves
to fully believe: We each can show the world,
so vast and vague, so small and specific,
we're much more than just an inevitable stone
and an empty honorific.

Dreaming Lisel Mueller

(8 February 1924 – 21 February 2020)

I dreamt Lisel Mueller on a train
the morning after I learned that she had passed.
She was riding through my present
to her past some 96 station stops away,
while I was rolling over into my next today.
If she saw me through the window
in my head, the one that opens wide
when my eyes finally slam shut,
she didn't show. She was busy
sorting petals of impatiens pink and white
she counted out like coins from an old purse.
The conductor in the aisle sidled up
with a smile, fingers snapping for the fare;
she handed him instead a book of verse.
When he asked how far she thought she'd get
on what she wrote, she answered
with a shrug and playful look. So like a poet,
don't you think, to find herself at last
on an endless train of words without a care,
and hoping for the smack of a hand on filmy glass
to let her know that she is finally there.

The Poet's Psalm

The Word is my Sherpa; it carries my craft.
   It leads me to heights from which I can see.
It gives me the clarity I need.
   It opens my soul.
It guides me through trails of thought
   for the sake of my sanity.

Even though I write in the blankness of verse,
   I will fear no trope,
for you are with me;
   your meaning and meter,
   they compose me.

You fill a page before me
   in the absence of my doubt;
you anoint my pen with ink;
   my mind overflows.
Surely your reason and rhyme shall lift
   each poem I submit,
and I shall dwell in some obscure anthology or other
   forever . . .or until I'm out-of-print.

Just Fishin'

I cut a hole in my mornings,
drop a line, hoping
to lift something of size
thrashing with vigor
onto the page — something
slick and silvery
in fresh light, dazzling.

Most times all I pull are minnows
from my murky depths.
Still, held close
and looked at
in just the right way,
some become whales
that swallow me whole.

Butchering a Poem

Like any good idea you've got to get a grip
before you start ripping into it. The better
the idea, the slicker it is slipping through
your hands, and once it's gone it's gone
for good, likely as not. So when you've got it
cornered, sitting still for a moment in mind,
grab that poem by the title if you can,
pin it to the page by leaning into that opening line
with whatever leverage you can find,
and work yourself into the spaces between words
feeling for the heart of it.

Somewhere between the fat and bone is muscle,
and if you can cut deft enough, trim the flab
without losing the sweet meat that makes
the best meaning, you'll find it: The living
soul of the thing that pulses through it
beginning to end, top to bottom. Find that
and you've got yourself the real deal.
Just make sure you have an idea worth the doing.
I know from experience:
It's easy to make a mess.

Wordsmithing

for Rolf

It's not as easy as it looks
forging words into poems,
pulling them from the fire
of the imagination and pounding them
into sound and syntax
with nothing but the hammers
of your fingertips striking
the keyboard of the computer.

You put a word to the anvil
of the page, try tapering it to fit
where you want in line
with other words
cooling in composition,
shaving letters and syllables
as needed, you never know
when a spark might ignite
a whole new idea
and you're scraping what
you've spent hours on
back into the cauldron
to begin again.

But when you get it right
you can practically smell it in the air,
see it on the face, it's there:
something smithed —
something real —
something that didn't exist
before you
with your labor
made from the molten metal
of your mind this thing
that you can read
and feel.

Wallflowers

Is there anything melancholier than a book unread?
All those words manufactured in someone's head, carefully
planned, revised, and designed on the page;
such a book vainly waits to engage, to entice
a curious hand to caress its spine — to cradle it, lift it
for a peek inside, opening it
to intimate interaction and flirtation,
inviting it to fulfill a sacred obligation . . .

Books unopened, unread, unspoken — shelved
to the side, boxed in corners — die in bits
each day they sit just gathering dust,
overlooked and out of the way.
They come into being teeming with grand expectations
of swirling society, even admiration,
only to find themselves pushed farther from notice
while others entertain a parade of suitors
held in their sway . . .

Time is unkind to the unused book, wasting away
with words unfulfilled. It yearns for more
than the attentions of its maker; it burns
for lovers, but spurned, sadly
learns to languish in a limbo of spent ambition,
lying in state between covers.

A Craving for Kumquats

The kumquat is a teardrop
of citrusy confusion.
No larger than a walnut really,
this fusion of orange and lemon
is fractured fruit turned inside-out,
its slim skin the candy, coating
an interior of acidic sour
you don't peel to reveal.
You chew through it all
for the sweet-sour flavor fully
to effect its magic on your tongue,
then swallow for the savor of the tart
to linger in the mouth and on your breath
before you start on the next one,
and the next after that,
until the handful that you had
is now gone.

A lot like life, this craving
for the kumquat —
to taste the measure of every pleasure
and leave nothing to waste.

You Say Tomato, I Say

Grow 'em
Pick 'em
Slice 'em
Lick 'em
Stir them into soup
Skin 'em
Crush 'em
Blend 'em
Mush 'em
Pound them into goop
Boil 'em
Freeze 'em
Fry 'em
Squeeze 'em
Let nothing go to waste
Can 'em
Jar 'em
Bag 'em
Store 'em
Reduce them to a paste
Love 'em
Crave 'em
Bought 'em
Ate 'em
Can't get me enough
Red vine
Brandywine
Big Beef
Early Girl
I'm addicted to this stuff
Black Plum
Cherry Buzz
Heirloom Green
Orange Jazz
Mmm, so good to munch
Indigo Beauty
Jubilee
Marizol Magic
Napoli
Are there any left for lunch?

October Rain

In Sturgeon Bay it's a bracing slap in the face:
light or lashing, mizzle or soak,
the rains of October feel different
from April's baptismal rinse
or May's maternal quenching.
What we get in October is a reminder,
cold and calculating,
that whatever pleasure we imbibed from July
and August's suddenly swollen technicolor skies
is just a black-and-white memory, brief relief
from heat that wants no part of a Door County fall.

Hot and Humid catch the express south
on September's zephyrs
and what we're left with on the thumb
is the chilling premonition in hand
that the razors of rain slashing us
as we dash from house to car or
car to store will soon enough morph
into needles of ice and more,
the long hard white blast of Wisconsin winter.

February in Wisconsin

My inner groundhog beseeches me
(mere hours after the pandemonium in Punxsutawney):
Forget that nonsense about sunlight and shadows —
burrow back under the covers and quilts!
If Winter has only six weeks left to rule,
its reign is going to be a terror
of slashing wind, blinding snow, and cutting cold.
Anyone thinking Spring will be riding to an early rescue
on zephyrs of sun-kissed warmth better brace themselves
for disappointment and frostbite:
February intends to exact revenge
for getting shorted its allotment of days
by taxing every last Covid-crazy one of us
the full measure of misery it can extract.

So. it's back to boots and gloves, long johns and layers
(trudging to the garage to coax the Toro back to life)
blow snow from one pile to another while plows
replace what was just cleared with their merciless blades.
It's back to fogged glasses and ice-slicked stairs
looking to knock us on our asses with one careless step
imprudently made. It's the litany
of wind chills and safety salt, traffic warnings
and school closings, slush puddles and black ice
on the stations of the cross-winds we must endure
to get us to a time of thaw and gradual greening.

Natives say a Wisconsin winter tests our patience
(and perseverance in the face of five months of numbing bleak)
week after week: The same slate gray landscape
ice-scraped by snow and wind, with February the fulcrum.
Get through *that* month, I'm told, a body can survive anything.
It's a test I've taken — and passed — again and again.
This year, though, I feel like chucking it all after one grim look,
go full groundhog, just sleep in.

Poesy Envy

for Tom Davis

I am stuck with the poems that brought me,
struck by how unseemly they seem
in the mixed company of an anthology,
as voluptuous verses scroll smartly on
decked in vogue vocabulary and stunning syntax,
hanging on the arms of authors who know
how to parade them to maximum effect
for the envious admiration of others
like me.

My ungainly companions look especially gaunt,
staring back at me with anguished expressions
as if I knew the answers to their questions:
Why are we *here?*
What have we *done?*
What do any of us *mean?*
They were content to reside in the closed
closet of accomplishment, comfortable
even in the obscurity of anonymity
when nothing more was expected of them
than an occasional public appearance
in a half-empty coffee house.
But now, ceremoniously pushed
into actual publication for all to see,
they seem pathetically under-dressed
and emphatically plain.

They hurl my words back at me
between the forced smiles and nimble niceties
of polite intercourse, deflecting compliments
with awkward grace and humility
(*We never imagined anything like this,*
they gawk), giving me the eye any time
one of mine wanders too freely to appraise
a comely couplet or seductive sonnet elsewhere.

You think we're miserable now, they hiss.
Just wait till later!
You'll be lucky to get a word out edgewise.

You'll be blocked for a month!

By the time we finish fitting into the Evening,
I am both humbled and grateful
to return to relative obscurity with my own,
which for better or worse are mine.
But my poems are bruised and defensive.
They wonder if they wouldn't sound better
in French? *Everything sounds better in French,*
they insist, and they fault me for not knowing that,
for not being sensitive to their dreams
of experiencing the flavors of a foreign tongue.
I try to ignore them, shrug my shoulders,
close the book. *I don't know French,* I say,
except, maybe, *C'est la vie?*

Ode to the Worm Moon

A moon by any other name
wouldn't sound so squirmy,
squiggling across the night sky
with white light bright as any
incandescent star we might surmise.
You are a beacon to the earth-
worms that heed your rise,
to crawl through crusts of crumb-
ling snow to find you reflected
on wet sidewalks and streets

(before finding themselves
squashed on the soles of feet).

You are the mother of moons
from which our rebirth sings,
and through your waxing
and waning our gibbous hearts
warm once more to the promises
of Spring. A worm by any other
moon wouldn't smell so sweet,
and no moon of any other night
could leave the season's first robins
such a morning delight.

Star Stuff(ed)

We are made of star stuff,
Carl Sagan said,
our every molecule of quiddity
celestial serendipity,
connecting us to matters
great and small,
vast and vaguely infinitesimal:

> We inhale the dust of our own
> creation with every breath
> we take, and exhale
> new planets and galaxies
> into the infinite promise of space.

Such a dawning thought
of what we might become,
if *become* is still within our reach.
Such a yawning waste
if what we've lately done
is all the legacy
we're likely to bequeath.

The Professional

I do my best work on my back,
in bed.
Words pour easily
into my hands from my head
when I'm in a demiurgic zone,
prone and processing,
and I'll tell you anything
I think you'll want to hear
while we're alone
just the two of us,
you accepting,
me giving,
the connection between us
somehow sinuous
as my fingers dance on keys
conjuring sounds
and silences too
in this act of communion
we share;

and I try to imagine
what you'll be feeling
as you fully take me in,
riding one rhythm
after another in time,
one rhyme leading
seductively to the next
as the act unwinds
beginning to end
in a gush of euphony
that brings you hopefully
back for more of me
maybe with one gnawing thought
nibbling the back of your mind:
how much of what I say is really me,
how much of what I don't
just the tease
of poetry?

An Ode to My Sesquipedalian Self

O wordy wordsmith within,
wantonly waxing deep
the logorrheic canyons of my mind,
I await the effusive torrents of your deluge
much like the gulch the flood that follows the storm!
Much like the maestro the symphonic euphony
that suddenly engulfs at the drop of his baton!
Abundance is paucity
compared to your unyielding yields.

You are Demeter to stingy Limos,
glorying in effulgent excess.
You are Plutus, horn full to overflowing,
blindly bestowing.
No settling for a word
when coils of clauses barely suffice!
No opting for a shriveled sentence or two
when whole paragraphs seem like haiku!

You, my sesquipedalian self, unleash
waves of words that wash away brevity
with tsunami-like verbosity,
filling every crevice of succinct silence,
every gap of pregnant pause,
with slabs of syllabication so deliriously dense
they stun the senses and twist the tongue.

More is never enough for you;
too much is much too little.
That is why such poets as I exist —
to drench the page with drivel.

A Miscellany of Family Matter

Living Out Loud

for any Orlocks everywhere

I'm not the kind for corners,
seeking the safety of shadows
from which to look into the light,
my voice muted lest I be disputed
for whatever words fly like birds
out my mind through my mouth.
I'm the one you hear
sometimes braying like an ass,
sometimes howling like a Ginsberg
in a crowded room, my voice
hollowing out a space, a place
from which my intonations
reverberate and boom.

I come from a long line of loud talkers
whose young are taught early on
to announce themselves through force
of lung, to fill silence with sound,
monotony with cacophony
until every black hole in conversation
is buzzing with white noise
spiked by eruption and detonation.
You want quiet instead of a riot,
spite us, don't invite us — we Orlocks
have spent generations living out loud,
perfecting the art of standing out
in any crowd, letting you know
our minds even when they're empty
as drums, banging in quick time
against time, until we're struck dumb.

My Name Goes Here

I was born wordless without
stance in this world
until my parents hung upon me
the combination of consonants and vowels
that became my identity — five syllables
broken down discretely, two/one/two,
spaced into three successive proper nouns
that bequeathed unto me an abundance
of euphony if not erudition.

The first begins with a closed-mouth *mm*
opening onto a high *ai* diphthong that
smacks face first into a digraph *K* sound consonant blend,
which kicks the word off a clef to a low and dulcet *ul*
that trills the air like my mother calling from the back door at dusk
(*my — kul*) to bring home this wayward one;
it almost sounds lyrical, doesn't it?

That is followed by a middle monohthong
(*jaan*) so nondescript it's barely mentioned
anymore except in formal introductions,
its rare public appearances these days limited
to applications and legal documentation,
where it's often reduced to a single letter.

The end is a conjunction/transitive verb made-up word
rumbling an *or* over a rolling *el* into an intractable *K*,
conducting my name to a sudden tumbling stop:

Michael John Orlock —

As if those three words could make sense of,
bring some semblance of order to,
the cacophony of chaos I was ceremoniously thrust into
one wintry March day in 1953.

Three words a birthright: Not quite totemic
in usage. Invoking them intentionally won't yield much
magic. Planting them in memory won't grow much of value.

But they were the first words I was given
and the last words I will leave
when this poem I am writing inevitably
ends.

How We Began

Once upon a time
we opened our arms to each other
on a sandy hill overlooking Lake Michigan.
The sky was a glaze of blue
baked in the kilns of August,
and I remember the way my shoes sank
in the shifting ground,
the way your dress snapped in the breeze
like a flag leading a parade.

I followed your finger
to a point on the horizon
where two sailboats seemed destined
to crash head-on and would have, too,
if the world lacked perspective.
Instead, they crossed one before the other
to become one ship with two bows,
frozen for an instant in line
like magic you conjured
out of everything with a smile.

Anniversary 2021

After 46 of these you'd think I'd know what words to choose
what words to use to conjure   capture   the content of time
that traces the line back to the moment you said *yes*
and I said *yes* and I became yours and you became mine

You'd think there'd be an expression could stretch that far
could thread through the days, the weeks, the months, the years
like a stitch so fine it's seamless to pull everything I want
to say together under one blanket of words warm with love

But I'm tongue-tied and speechless still   stumbling and stupefied
after all this accumulation of life we've lived together   together
in each other's shadows moving through time   that you said *I do*
one January day in 1975 and made everything I wished for
and wanted and dreamed for and needed come true.

My While's Worth

for Liz

I value my while.
I put a premium price on whiling away,
so it makes perfect sense
my while should be worth a lot to me,
especially now in these autumn years
of pandemic and political pestilence
when everything seems to scream by
at twice the speed of a blur.

Compounded daily in the present
tense of exchange, I figure my while is worth
at least as much as the next guy's
and twice what it was yesterday
when I spent awhile whiling away while
waiting for the world to take a surprising turn.

Then you showed up as expected as today
while all that whiling was wasting away,
and with wiles that have nothing to do
with the while I was whiling with,
you gave me something worth
all the while I was waiting for:

The Typography of Sleep

Each night beside me
under warm quilts and sheets
(you furled like a wayward tilde ~
against my virtual/virgule)
we sleep —

We've done this so many times now
we punctuate each other's rest
just by sensing, the choreography
of touch and turn, slip and stretch
the typography of our dreaming.

We compose ourselves thus nightly
anew and come morning
awake to a next day in hand,
curled in an impromptu &
(ampersand):

Beautiful Magic

for Rosi, who is

Nature needs no wand to cast
spells of beguiling green,
nor a hat from which to pull rabbits
by the dozens, nibbling new shoots
shot from the earth like a shock
of flowers from up the sleeve
of my garden. April might
delight in a bit of misdirection,
getting me to see one thing marvelous
in bright morning sun
before sawing the day in half
with a blast of winter cold;
and May enjoys her sleight-of-hand, too,
conjuring bouquets of tulips
from behind my back
wherever I look; but the trick
that dazzles most is the simplest:
Hypnotizing me (easy me, willing me!)
to believe once again the magic of things
seeing the world through your eyes
come Spring.

Goofballs

I couldn't carry a tune
if it came equipped with handles
but Addie makes me want to sing
nonsense songs that use her name
in nonsense rhymes that make her laugh
to melodies that lurch like zombies
cobbled together from memory
of songs I've heard or think I've heard
but probably haven't anyway
it makes no never mind to Addie
she just laughs out loud longer
the more ridiculous I sound
mangling words and rhythm to end
in exaggerated falsetto *eee*'s
that scrape against the ceiling
before crumbling into bass rumblings so low
her laugh becomes a choral tremolo
which only encourages me to sing louder
until maybe Mom or Dad or Grandma
or one of Addie's big sisters warily
peeks in to see what the ruckus is all about:

Just Grandpa and Addie
one of them might shout
two goofy kids doing goofy things
on the kind of day
that makes goofballs want to sing.

Baby Cakes

Kayla teases with a smile.
Her smile is the frosting
of her face, a smear of sweet
too sweet to resist, and this
is something we both know:

At five years old and counting
she is already accomplished
in the art of collecting hearts
just by flirting, skirting
the chair where I sit
trying to read the morning paper
and concentrate on a television
program, poking her face
in front of yesterday's news
or dancing in circles
in front of the screen,
gyrating to music maybe
only she can hear.

I call her name for quiet
and some semblance of order
but she just laughs, laughs
in that way little girls have
of laughing at the absurdities
of old men with their newspapers
and pre-game analysis
of meaningless football games,
because she knows already
that a smile is enough
to get her what she wants
if not everything she needs,
and teasing her grandpa
is the quickest way to get it,
easy as licking frosting
off a slice of cake--

And I think, What will this girl be
like when she's twenty and counting

and what hearts will melt
in the radiance of that smile
as mine melts again, now?

Mimpsy

Mimpsy is as Mimpsy does
with whimsy and full wonder.
At ninety-two, in years and weight,
you'd think she'd act her number.

But Mimpsy isn't one to stoop
to dotage at this juncture;
the days are bright, her step still light,
with limits left to puncture.

So, hug that little bony frame
and don't hold back another,
for Mimpsy's made of sturdy stuff —
after all, she is my mother.

Ride, Janie, Ride

for my sister, forever strong

My sister Jane isn't tall
she just seems so
standing up on stage
in the middle of the merriment
of *Ride, Janie, Ride 2019*
her annual fundraiser
in the fight against cancer
that brings nearly a thousand
motorcycles   mostly Harley's
rumbling off the highway
in double-breasted formation
like some improvised army
into the vast parking lots
of Skooters   a big box saloon
and entertainment emporium
out in the sticks west of Joliet.

Her slight shoulders square
as she surveys the crowd
circling the stage
lots of leather vests
big hair and deep pockets
wondering where the music went
as she accepts the microphone
and gets to the point.

I'm here because of you! she says
her voice surprisingly louder
than one of the cut-exhaust softtails
outside leaning in the lot.
But there's more to do!

Thirteen years ago
she got mugged by a gang
of abnormal cells
that decided to pick a fight with her.
The family doctor metastasized into a team
and the prognosis was grim:
no way a woman so small

could carry on too long
with stage four lymphoma
ripping her insides out.

Yet here she is   still
pitching hardball
for any hard cash people
can spare people
who need the help:
kids with cancer
families buried under bills
lives suddenly reduced
to the most basic equation
serious sickness imposes:
put up or shut up for good.

This Harley crowd puts up
hundreds of thousands
to fund the fight another year.
Meanwhile

Cancer can't shut up Jane.
Not yet.
There's still too much life
left to live in her.
Too much sass.
Too much spunk.
I know my sister.

Cancer picked on the wrong girl.

Petey

lopes through life in leaps and sprints
bounding after balls with hairpin twists
never stopping at stairs or chairs
but seemingly soaring through astonished air
until what he's after is caught and brought
back to the spot where he began
to begin the chase again and again.

A white mutt with a whiff of dalmatian
somewhere in his pedigree,
Petey is distinguished by a brownish blot
at the base of his tail and black ears
that flop in alternation
with each vigorous shake of his head.
There's pit bull in his blood, too;
you can see it in his fearsome jaw
and the wide set of his pale eyes
but really Petey is a pussy cat in disguise;
he likes nothing better than
to curl on a lap for belly rubs
and back scratches instead.

A rescue dog from a kill shelter in Green Bay,
Petey is proof — love is the wrapping
for the gift of life without a moment
to waste in despair, not when there
are balls to chase and rooms to run
and time to play without care.

Dealing

for Sammie, 2009 – 2020

We know what we're getting into.
It's part of the deal, an agreement
as old as our species together
when we came to an arrangement
sometime in our primordial past
that has benefited us both:

For food, shelter, fresh water
and occasional exercise,
for grooming and basic health care,
the occasional treat and toy
for good measure, access to the sofa
and the most comfortable spot
at the foot of the bed or that
accommodating crevice between us
in our nightly slumber, you give
unconditional devotion and that look
in the liquid depths of your eyes,
lets us glimpse the best of ourselves
limitless as the stars in the sky.

But knowing the terms doesn't lessen
the pain that comes when the deal expires,
the pain that wells within us when
we remember the sounds of you
or we stare at the now empty spaces
you made yourself home. Nature
has tethered you to a different clock
that calls your name decades perhaps
before we hear our own. What's left
in the silence of your leaving is grieving,
and a celestial certainty that pierces the heart:
Nothing made of mortal flesh can last.
So hold fast, dear friend, and wait.
Where you go now, we follow.

Endings

In Praise of Bastard Toadflax

Is there any flower more essentially elementally American than you?
You thrive where others shrivel and die. Bruised by cold
or baked by heat, you flourish nevertheless, hardier
and scrappier than weeds. You are complete unto yourself.

Your petal-less buds are proletarian in their economy. Your berries
feed the hungry and wanting in a season of need. No brides
prize you for their engagements; no florists devise arrangements
around you. Your name is your pedigree, without pretense
or shame. Let the rose regale itself in its remote beauty!
Let the orchid pamper itself in its aristocratic frailty!

They are exceptions but you are the rule. Like Steinbeck's
stubborn dirt-poor Okies, you abide, tough bastard that you are.
And like a plague of Old Testament toads, you're everywhere,
unabashedly bursting from sea to surging sea.

Climbing Hills
with Amanda Gorman

There's no mistaking us, even from a distance:
You're feisty, female and remarkably young,
slight as a sprig of California cosmos
lifting your beautiful face to the sun, and I,
I am a redundancy — a Midwestern man
middle in most metrics but senior of age,
common as a weed clinging to a curbside; yet
we are one,
you climbing your hills, me climbing mine
that roll across this great land from ocean to ocean,
to see from the summits what words have done,
what words can still do.

For it is words that connect us,
me and you,
in ways too tangible to ignore,
words that feed us, fill us, heal us and more;
words that mix your story with mine, words
that make us unmistakably American.
They pour from minds and mouths and pens
into the unfinished manuscript that is
this country, 'tis of thee and me and all poets
unknown or renowned, forgotten or celebrated,
who have ever raised their voices to sing
a line or two in the chorus of this ambitious poem
of ours more than 243 years in the writing.

Whatever hills you climb, Ms. Gorman,
going forward, know the words you carry with you
are the words carried forth from
all of us,
passed from Wheatley to Whitman to Sandburg to Frost,
Dickinson to Brooks to Angelou to Smith
and multitudes of others, entrusted to you
for their power and promise of inspiration.
Let them ring and sing free for all to hear
at any distance, lifting us to new heavens
alongside you on voices of shared jubilation.

An Opuscule of Diminishing Scale

*opuscule: n. a small or minor literary work or musical
composition*

Some poems tower on the power of soaring imagination.
Some achieve new glory in sheaves of critical examination.
Others have the pluck of luck to use their limitations
to find a niche in trendy kitsch with homey invocation.
The best are those that blend a dose of cunning innovation
with a splash of balderdash and familiar replication.

This tome is a different poem: It has no scope or scale.
No matter how it's measured, it's a minnow not a whale.
It doesn't seek successfully to even somewhat fail
to make itself more memorable than forgettable junk mail.
It simply is a feckless fizz of worthless words inveigled
arranged in ways to dull and daze those who read retail.

And if you've got (or maybe not) this far to line thirteen
to contemplate the aggregate of what these words might mean,
to seek to find in soul or mind that something left unseen
but surely hidden there somewhere for *you* to truly glean,
it is my task (before you ask) to preface line eighteen —
there's nothing in the ending that wasn't there between.

About Your Author

Mike Orlock is a retired high school teacher and coach. He enjoys travel, reading, writing, films, and spending time with his two children and five grandchildren. His short fiction has appeared in *TriQuarterly*, the literary journal of Northwestern University, and *Another Chicago Magazine*. His poetry has appeared online in "Your Daily Poem" website, in the WFOP yearly calendars, *Verse Wisconsin*, the *Los Angeles Times*, the *Blue Heron Review*, the *Peninsula Pulse*, and various other venues. He has published three other books of poetry: *You Can Get Here from There: Poems of Door County & Other Places; Poetry Apocalypse & Selected Verse;* and *Mr. President! Poetry, Polemics & Fan Mail from Inside the Divide.* His work has been awarded by the Illinois Arts Council, the Wisconsin Writers Association, and the Wisconsin Fellowship of Poets. In 2021, he was named Poet Laureate of Door County.